W9-BKC-995

FINDING HOPE

Additional Books by the Authors

RONNA FAY JEVNE

*No Time for Nonsense**
It All Begins with Hope
*Striving for Health**
Voice of Hope
*When Dreams Don't Work**
*Key Elements of Hope-Focused Counselling**
*co-authored

~

JAMES E. MILLER

What Will Help Me? / How Can I Help?
When You're Ill or Incapacitated / When You're the Caregiver
How Will I Get Through the Holidays?
One You Love Is Dying
When You Know You're Dying
Winter Grief, Summer Grace
Autumn Wisdom
The Caregiver's Book
Welcoming Change
A Pilgrimage Through Grief
Helping the Bereaved Celebrate the Holidays
A Little Book for Preachers
Effective Support Groups
The Rewarding Practice of Journal Writing
One You Love Has Died

~

FINDING HOPE

Ways to See Life in a Brighter Light

Ronna Fay Jevne
and
James E. Miller

To Dad, for your gift of vision and your years of caring,
and to Glen, for your life of hope and your years of friendship.

To Mike, for being a living example of hope through the years.

We are indebted to a number of people who have assisted in various ways in the creation of this book. They include Clare Barton, Beth Beams, Chris Crawford, Sue Devito, Wendy Edey, Jim Gurnett, Carrie Hackney, Jennifer Levine, Christen Miller-Rieman, Natasha Robinson, and Don Swanson, as well as the board, staff, and volunteers of the Hope Foundation of Alberta and Ronna's 1998 class of *Hope and the Helping Relationship*. We are each especially grateful to our spouses, Allen and Bernie, for their endless hours of discussion and their living proof of the power of hope.

Photographs by James E. Miller

Copyright © 1999 by Willowgreen Publishing

All rights reserved. No part of this book may be reproduced or transmitted in any form or by any means, electronic or mechanical, including photocopying, recording, or by any information and retrieval systems, without permission in writing from the publisher.

Willowgreen Publishing
PO Box 25180
Fort Wayne, Indiana 46825
219/424-7916
www.willowgreen.com

Library of Congress Catalogue
Card Number: 98-94922

ISBN 1-885933-30-4

"Hope" is the thing with feathers –
That perches in the soul –
And sings the tune without words –
And never stops – at all –

EMILY DICKINSON

~

Foreword

Hope is amazing. You can't touch it, but you can definitely feel it. You can't physically see it by itself, but you can hold it and carry it. Hope doesn't weigh anything, but it can ground you and anchor you.

Hope is paradoxical. You can live under extremely adverse conditions and have a great deal of hope. You can have everything seemingly going right in your life and yet have little or no hope at all. You can be dangerously ill and very hopeful at the same time. You can even be dying and have much you're looking forward to. On the other hand, you can be the picture of health and wonder if you can find the energy to hope for anything.

There is no substitute for hope. Joy and laughter may help it but they cannot replace it. Closeness and love may encourage it but they cannot duplicate it. Only hope itself can hope. Only hope itself can hang on.

Our deep respect for hope has led us to create this book. Hope has played a central role in our lives as individuals and it has been the backbone of our work as professionals. Ronna has become a leading authority on hope through her work as a researcher, university professor, and psychologist. Jim has made hope a central theme in his work as a minister, grief counselor, and photographer.

The two of us had never met before writing this book. We were familiar with each other's work from a distance, but we knew almost nothing about one another personally. From his home in Fort Wayne, Indiana, Jim telephoned Ronna and asked if he could interview her. From her home in Edmonton, Alberta, Ronna responded, "Why don't you spend a few days with my husband Allen and me and we'll talk?" So Jim hopped a plane and talk we did.

We talked about our experience as professionals. We reviewed the research on hope. We shared our own struggles as individuals. We confirmed the unquestionable necessity of hope in daily life, as well as in times of adversity.

What surprised us was the consistency and yet the simplicity of the ways people use hope to see life in a brighter light. We agreed that hope is not dependent on advanced technical skills. It does not require physical strength or moral purity. No discipline or trade can claim it as their sole domain. Hope develops and is strengthened by relatively obvious and somewhat modest endeavors.

In the pages that follow, we share some of the ways you can invite hope into your own life. If in some small way your understanding of hope is deepened, or if your experience of hope is strengthened, our purpose will have been accomplished.

Ronna Jevne
Jim Miller

There never was night that had no morn.

DINAH MARIA MULOCK CRAIK

~

The word which God has written
in the brow of every person is hope.

VICTOR HUGO

~

It is hope which makes the shipwrecked sailor
strike out with his arms in the midst of the sea,
though no land is in sight.

OVID

~

No one wants to hear the words, "There is no hope." None of us wants to be in the situation of saying, "I feel hopeless." In difficult times we want to sense that hope is nearby, or at least at the end of the tunnel. Whether the challenge that confronts us is illness or disability, separation from a loved one or the loss of something very important to us, our situation is eased if we feel at least some hope.

You might notice in your own life that you use the word "hope" often but you have not thought much about what hope is. When it comes right down to it, you can't easily describe hope. You may not be sure exactly what it means. You are not alone. Even the scholars have been unable to agree on a definition. No one, however, doubts the value of hope. No one questions that life is difficult without it.

We know there are two basic situations that lead to feelings of hopelessness – uncertainty and captivity. With uncertainty we fear that things will change in some way we do not want. In captivity we fear that things will not change as we feel they need to. In both cases it seems we have lost control of our future.

Lack of hope is most visible in the person whose days seem lifeless and long, the person we commonly think of as discouraged or depressed. Yet there are many people who struggle silently with hopelessness in the midst of busy and demanding schedules. Life for them has become a treadmill of obligations. It has lost its satisfaction. They feel trapped by circumstance and sense that their future will be an endless rut of meaningless activity.

Difficulty and uncertainty are part of life for all of us at one time or another. The question becomes how we can sustain our hope during such times. How can we build hope when ours gets low, and how can we find hope when it has disappeared?

As authors, we have no way of knowing if you picked up this

book in search of enhancing your own hope or the hope of someone special to you. We don't know if you're wanting to find hope, keep your hope, or build your hope. Then again, you may have selected this book out of mere curiosity. By answering some commonly-asked questions and by offering some specific suggestions, we hope this book will serve your purpose, whatever that is.

What *is* hope?

Hope is looking forward with both confidence and unsureness to something good. When we hope, we anticipate that something we want to happen can indeed happen. Even if it's unlikely, it's still possible. Even if others do not see things as we do, we're still convinced what we hope for can come true. Will it happen for sure? No one can say. Yet even when it's unlikely, that is no reason for us to stop hoping. It is no reason to surrender the future we have envisioned.

When we hope, we expect the future can somehow be better, no matter what our present condition is. And should that future turn out to be other than we imagined, all is not lost. For when we hope, the present is also affected. We can still help create a tomorrow we're prepared to be a part of, even if that tomorrow looks different than we presumed it would. We can still find meaning in what our days hold, even if it may take us awhile to see our situation in a new light.

As much as anything, hope helps us live with the unpredictability we must face from time to time in our lives. It serves as a companion when the future is unsure or unclear. Hope stays with us and heartens us when our options appear limited. When the possibilities seem to diminish, it harkens us to see life as it may become.

Is hoping the same as wishing?

No, they're very different. Wishing is passive. All you have to do when you wish for something is think it: "I wish I had a million dollars." For the most part, wishing doesn't really believe your dream will come true. Hoping, on the other hand, is more active. It requires your personal involvement, even if that means that what you're to do is "actively wait." Hoping takes effort.

Neither is hoping the same as coping. When you cope, you try to adapt. You do what you can to get by. You concentrate on fixing a problem or finding a solution. You can be coping and not believe the future will be any better. Hoping remains open to *all* the possibilities, including the possibility that things may turn out other than you imagined and it can still be okay. And life has many examples of situations actually turning out better than could have been expected or imagined.

Hope is not just something you believe or feel or do. It involves believing, feeling, and doing – and much more. It includes every part of you – your mind, body, heart, and soul.

Why hope?

We hope because it is essential to the quality of our life – as essential as is breath to our physical existence. When we hope, we are willing to get up one more time than we fall down. We are willing to give ourselves one more chance, again and again.

Hope sets our sail in difficult seas, or even becomes the anchor as we wait out a storm. When the winds of fate blow us off course, we are not entirely lost. We have some idea what we must do and we tack our way back to shore.

With hope we can deepen as a human being. With hope we can find meaning in how we respond to what has happened to us. In other words, with hope, whatever the outcome, we can go on.

Does everyone hope?

Yes, everyone is born to hope. It comes naturally. We all start out with that capacity. It is easier to continue to hope if we have grown up having our basic needs met. If, however, we have had one disappointment in life after another, it becomes harder to trust that the future will include some of what we hope for. But we can still learn and re-learn how to hope, whatever has happened to us.

Is hope the same for everyone?

No, each of us hopes differently. We are as distinctive in how we hope as in how we look or talk or act. Some of us hope quickly, almost reflexively. Others of us hope more slowly and gradually. Some of us are bold in how we hope, while others hope more quietly and tentatively.

We tend to hope as we have lived. Our successes give us more confidence to hope. We hope with more assurance when we realize the many ways we can influence the future. Even our failures can strengthen our hope, if we learn from them, and if we feel supported as we go through them. We also become more confident hopers when we realize some hopes take more than one attempt before they're fulfilled.

It helps if we have had a "mentor of hope" – someone who models hope for us, someone who believes in us and hopes with us and for us. This person is an exemplar of how to become a hopeful person ourselves. Without such a mentor, the challenge to hope is greater, but still very possible.

When we're around negative people, we tend to learn to be less hopeful. It becomes psychologically safer to do so. We start expecting things not to turn out as we want. That way we're less likely to get hurt.

Does everyone always hope?

No. Hope fluctuates for every person. We can experience more or less of it on any given day or during any given period. We each have our own rhythm of hope. Sometimes it's only natural for our hope to go down. That happens most often in situations in which we feel trapped or powerless.

When our hope feels weak, that doesn't mean that *we* are weak. This is not a deficiency on our part or a sign that we've done something wrong. It's nothing to be ashamed of. Many people have wrestled with low hope for long periods of time while still leading meaningful and productive lives. Albert Schweitzer had bouts of discouragement throughout his adulthood. So did Abraham Lincoln. Writer Virginia Woolf, composers Handel and Mahler, and entertainers Joan Rivers and Rod Steiger have all felt hope's absence at a very deep level and yet left their unique marks on the world. You probably have people in your own life who could tell you of a time gone by when their hope felt precariously low, and how they wondered if it would ever return.

Hope can go down or go away for various reasons. Demanding or depressing situations that continue for a long time can fatigue our hope. Times of illness or unwanted change are particularly hard on it. Sometimes it's a grief that goes on and on, or a disappointment, or a heartbreak. A series of trying experiences, one after another, can wear down our hope. We don't have time to rebound from one episode before we're hit with another.

Our hope can also be damaged. Often the cause is not so much a major event as it is a harsh word or a thoughtless gesture when we're feeling especially vulnerable. Changes in our bodies can affect our hope too. Chemical imbalances can occur as a result of illness or aging. Side effects of medications can also disturb hope. Then again, there may be no apparent reason for our hope to decline, at least none we can identify. Usually the cause will make itself known in time.

If I am low on hope or feel I have no hope, can my hope return?

Yes, it can, unquestionably. Sometimes it is as if our hope has gone into hiding and one day it re-emerges. Other times it is like our hope has been injured. As with any physical injury, time and effort and caring can help restore it. Just as we may need to do some things to help our body recover, we may need to participate in the recovery of our hope if it is to heal. Sometimes we can do that ourselves, and other times we will benefit from the assistance of others. Reading and applying what we read can also help. Ultimately though, it is each of us who must make the choice to reclaim our hope. It is not just handed to us. We must reach for it.

Does it take work to hope or is it fun to do?

Yes and yes.

Yes, hope often takes work, even a great deal of work. Sometimes you must struggle against the odds. Sometimes you have to stand alone. Sometimes you're misunderstood in what you're doing. Sometimes hoping takes more energy than you're sure you have to give. Sometimes it even hurts to hope. It's a risk you take. But hoping has many more potential benefits than it has detriments.

And yes, it can be fun to hope too. You can feel encouraged as you begin to do it. It can feel gratifying as you become good at it. The results of your hoping can be rewarding – *very* rewarding. Not only does the future become brighter; today feels brighter. The effects upon yourself and others can be energizing. You may be surprised about the support you receive, the inspiration you find, and the inspiration you give others.

Here's the critical question: how do I learn to hope?

There are various ways you can learn to find, keep, and build hope. Some ways will work better for you than others. The only way you'll know which ones work for you is by trying. Some ways will work better on certain days or at certain stages of your life. You'll figure it out as you go along. We've compiled a sampling of ideas to guide you on your way. Many more possibilities exist than we've included here. Start with the basics and build from there.

We've written this book so you can take your time as you read it. We encourage you not to hurry through it. Reflect upon the ideas about hope as you come across them. As you move from page to page, think about your own experiences in life – both what has happened to you in the past and what's happening to you now. Spend time with the photographs we've provided and the quotations we've selected. Consider reading only a few pages at a sitting or perhaps a single section a day. If you keep a journal, use it as you read these pages. Maybe you'll want to read what's here with another person or to another person. Maybe you'll want to talk with a friend or partner about the responses you have, the memories you uncover, and the hopes you find or build.

Know that our hope as authors is for your hope to be as strong as possible.

If you do not hope,
you will not find what lies beyond your hopes.

CLEMENT OF ALEXANDRIA

~

From a little spark may burst a mighty flame.

DANTE ALIGHIERI

~

Hope is the physician of every misery.

IRISH PROVERB

~

Throw the hope switch.

Imagine it's evening and a storm has knocked out the electricity at home. Sure, you can use candles for awhile. But you'd like the lights to come back on, and sooner rather than later. So what do you do? You make sure the wall switch is flipped on so that when the power returns, so will the light. Unless you throw that switch, the current won't get through.

Hope works the same way. Unless you "throw the hope switch," allowing any hope out there to flow your way, it won't. It can't. The circuit isn't complete.

So how do you flip on your hope switch? You open to the possibility that hope exists somewhere, however hopeless or hopeful you feel at the moment. You accept that hope is real and it works, whether you can prove it or not. You admit that hope can play a vital role in people's lives, whether it does in yours right now or not.

You throw the hope switch when you acknowledge that the future is uncertain, which means that it can go in more than one direction. Consequently, it's possible for things to turn out *better* than you expect as well as worse than you wish. You throw that switch when you say, "I think hope is within the realm of possibility. I may not be sure how or when I'll have it, but I won't rule it out of my life forever." You trip that switch when you pick up a book about hope and remain receptive to what it has to say.

Have you thrown your hope switch? If not, will you do so before you turn this page? Whether or not you hope at the moment, will you at least hope to hope?

The sunrise never failed us yet.

CELIA THAXTER

~

My heart leaps when I behold
A rainbow in the sky.

WILLIAM WORDSWORTH

~

One laugh of a child
will make the holiest day more sacred still.

ROBERT INGERSOLL

~

Notice signs of hope.

A wonderful thing about hope is that it's all over the place. You don't have to manufacture it – it's already present. Often you don't have to search for it – all you have to do is look in its direction. It's just as evident in the simple as in the grand, in the nearby as in the faraway.

An easy place to notice hope is in nature. The color, the beauty, and the grandeur can be inspiring. Nature's enormous diversity offers this reminder: "There are *many* possibilities." Look quietly and thoughtfully at individual creations – maple leaves and daffodils, sea shells and butterfly wings – and you can see nature suggesting, "An Unseen Hand is at work."

Some signs of hope are dramatic – a glowing sunrise, a vivid rainbow, a bright piece of artwork, a hot air balloon making its way heavenward. Other signs of hope are quieter – the way bark heals on a tree, the way illness heals in a body, or the way hurt heals in a soul. Hope is on display when people dream together and then work to make those dreams come true. It's seen when people embrace one another, and forgive one another, and help one another.

Hope is just a glance away when you look into the face of a newborn or a child, when you view the face of anyone who loves, and when you gaze into the eyes of an older person who is passionate about life. You can see sure signs of hope in those who willingly risk, those who unselfishly give, those who courageously start over.

Today, just observe what's going on around you. Pay attention to any signs of hope you see. Wherever you are, they're there. Whatever is happening, you can catch a glimpse of them. The question is, will you?

A true friend is one soul in two bodies.

ARISTOTLE

~

The ear is the road to the heart.

VOLTAIRE

~

I thank you for your voices: thank you:
Your most sweet voices.

WILLIAM SHAKESPEARE

~

Listen to voices of hope.

He confessed to his friend his fear that he was about to give in to his addiction. His friend's voice was quiet yet sure: "You've come so far. I believe you have it in you to keep going."

Deep in grief, she wondered aloud if she could ever feel happy again. The woman across the table, herself a widow, said, "It took longer than I expected for joy to return. But it did. I'm convinced it will return to you too."

Voices of hope say things like "I believe in you," "You have it in you," and "Yes, you can." Such voices offer assurances that are grounded in truth. The person who's speaking really *does* believe, really *does* see the possibility. They may even have *lived* that possibility. Maybe it's not a sure thing, but there's certainly plenty of reason to hope.

The strongest voices of hope come from people you respect and people who respect you. Some voices come from those who have already died but whose messages have not. Sometimes hopeful voices are in poems and stories and books that touch you at your core. A thought from a letter, a song, or a piece of scripture can speak deeply to you.

Sometimes voices of hope don't involve words at all. When the respected newspaper editor Jacobo Timerman was a political prisoner in Argentina in the 1970's, he was placed in solitary confinement. Through a peephole he could see a fellow prisoner across the hall staring back through his own peephole. The man would place his nose before the tiny window, lightly rub it, then place his eye there and point to it. He did this over and over. Timerman understood the message: "Tenderness will one day reappear." That silent assurance gave him great hope.

Listen to those voices, whatever form they take, that encourage and confirm and uplift you. They have something important to say. Even more, they have something real and true to say.

O for yesterdays to come!

EDWARD YOUNG

~

Study the past,
if you would divine the future.

CONFUCIUS

~

We must never despair;
our situation has been compromised before,
and it has changed for the better;
so I trust it will again.

GEORGE WASHINGTON

~

Look back.

Your life is a story. As such, it has a cast of characters, a series of settings, and a plot that unfolds. There are ups and downs in your story, twists and turns, predictable events and surprises. At the heart of the story of your life is another one – the story of your hope. Sometimes you have to look back to see it.

Your hope story is unquestionably unique. No one else has lived your life. You've had your own trials, your own troubles, your own sorrows. But you've also had your satisfactions, your successes, your joys. You've had your own reasons to live, your own occasions to love.

It may be that this is a time of seemingly invincible hope for you. It's also possible that something has happened and right now your hope is low, perhaps lower than you've ever known. It may be a time when it's hard to believe you'll ever feel good again, or you'll ever be yourself again. You may feel hope has slipped away and left you, never to return. If this is the case, could you, for now, simply accept that's what you're feeling? Feeling this way is more common than you may think. It happens to many, many people.

Looking back can help. Think about a time in your life when you felt especially hopeful. Take a moment right now. What was that time like? What were you thinking and doing? What were you hoping for? What were you excited about? Now carry those feelings into the present.

Whether or not you feel hopeful now, you can feel hopeful again. Why? Because you've done it before. You've had the experience of hope. You've got the makings. You can remember what it's like.

By looking back in this way, you take a step toward looking forward. By remembering, you start anticipating.

Opportunities are seldom labelled.

John A. Shedd

~

Let your hook be always cast.
In the stream where you least expect it,
there will be fish.

Ovid

~

Life is a series of surprises,
and would not be worth taking or keeping
if it were not.

Ralph Waldo Emerson

~

Expect to find hope where you least expect it.

Jack's fingernails were falling out. He was in constant pain. He questioned if he could tolerate any more treatment for his cancer. One especially depressing day a five-year-old boy approached Jack's hospital bed. Like Jack, he was both bald and weak from his chemotherapy treatments. He held out a broken toy and said cheerfully, "Mister, could you fix this for me?" In that instant Jack decided that if this little guy could push ahead with hope, so could he. Ten years after that boy entered his room, Jack is still going strong.

Sometimes when life spirals downward or when it hits bottom, something unexpected happens. Someone enters your life for a few moments and because of what they say or do, you're drawn to hope again. Perhaps a friend goes out of their way to connect with you and you're suddenly reminded you're not alone, and an energy begins to grow within you. Maybe you come upon something that gives you a positive jolt. The 19th century German physicist Gustav Fechner found his long-term depression suddenly eased when he was stopped short one day by an amazingly beautiful flower bed. He later said that moment of serendipity was the turning point in his healing.

You can come upon hope in places you wouldn't predict, in people you'd least expect, through events you'd never anticipate. More often than not, hope comes to you through ordinary experiences on ordinary days. Often the words are not particularly special, although they may become unusually special to you. The moment is not long-lasting, but it lasts long enough. You're caught unaware, and the next thing you know, hope is right in front of you. If it's not blossoming, at least it's budding. And somehow you sense that it will one day be a truly beautiful bloom.

Expect to come upon hope when you're least expecting it. Often it's not a matter of your finding hope – hope may find you.

The hardest step is that over the threshold.

JAMES HOWELL

~

The beginning is half the whole.

ARISTOTLE

~

Unless you call out
who will open the door?

CONGOLESE PROVERB

~

Break the silence.

She quit talking when she was eight. Something traumatic and embarrassing had happened to Maya Angelou, who would grow up to be a world-famous poet. After her silence had gone on for a long time, the most beautiful and sophisticated woman in Maya's small hometown invited the child into her home. Over lemonade, she read to Maya and explained that poetry was music written for the human voice. She encouraged the child to read poetry aloud to herself, which Maya did, first while hidden under her mother's bed and then out in the open. Later she began to write and recite her own poetry, expressing what she felt. Her true voice returned.

A silence often accompanies times of low hope or no hope. You may impose that silence on yourself or others around you may do it. Sometimes our culture encourages silence, preaching that we should always be happy, acting as if nothing were the matter, even when it is not true. This can be a problem for anyone, but even more so for a person who struggles with hope. People around you may not know what to say or do. Feeling uncomfortable, they may say and do nothing at all, deepening the silence. You may contribute to silencing yourself by running restlessly from activity to activity, never slowing down. You may work too hard or too long. You may numb yourself with addictive substances. You may protect yourself by keeping a distance from others. In doing any of these things, you keep a distance from yourself. You collaborate in the silence.

There is only one solution: break the silence. This takes effort and courage. It takes saying in your own way, "Today I am low on hope," or "What I am facing seems hopeless." You may break your silence by opening up to another or by writing for yourself. You may break it by being very honest in prayer. However you do it, when you break this silence, you take a giant step in the right direction. You head toward hope.

Nature has created humankind
to no other end
but to lend and to borrow.

FRANCOIS RABELAIS

~

We should not moor a ship with one anchor,
or our life with one hope.

EPICTETUS

~

Borrow hope.

He felt he was at the end of his rope. His career lay shattered. His marriage was ending. He had no money. His future looked dark and bleak. Over coffee at a diner he said to his friend, "I'm afraid I've lost my hope." Paul responded, "Then you can use mine until yours returns."

She knew her chances were slim. A risky surgery was her only possibility. She realized she needed more hope if her body was to have every chance it needed. So she called Audrey. While Audrey found the request unusual, she readily agreed to loan every ounce of hope she had. The day of the operation and for many days afterward, it was *two* people's hopes that led to healing.

You do not have to possess your own hope in order to have hope. You do not have to rely solely and completely on your personal resources. Hope can come on loan from others. Borrowing hope from another person doesn't deplete that hope at all. It's just as full as ever, and sometimes fuller. And borrowed hope can be just as effective as hope that's generated in the moment. In short, borrowed hope works. We, the authors, know this ourselves. The two stories above are our own.

Of course, you're not limited to borrowing your hope from people around you. You can borrow it from those far away, even from those no longer living. You can gather hope from the promises of your beliefs, whether that involves a particular religious faith or your personal sense of spirituality. You can temporarily use the hope you find in songs, readings, stories, movies, even dreams.

Borrow all the hope you want, whenever you want, for as long as you want. When the time is right, you can lend it too.

A life spent making mistakes
is not only more honorable but more useful
than a life doing nothing.

GEORGE BERNARD SHAW

~

Start by doing what's necessary,
then what's possible,
and suddenly you are doing
the impossible.

FRANCIS OF ASSISI

~

Experiment.

His hope was back! When asked what had helped restore it, Tom listed a litany of efforts from medication to meditation. "However, the real change in my hope," he said, "was when I started swimming."

There is no single right way to foster hope or to discover hope. There are *many* right ways. What works best for others may not work best for you. What works well at any given moment in time may change as you change or your life changes.

Perhaps you've relied on your achievements to buoy you and now you can't perform as you once did. Will you explore new ways to add meaning to your life? Perhaps a nourishing relationship has ended. What will you now do to nurture yourself and to share your nurturing with others? Perhaps being in nature has always invigorated you and suddenly you're confined indoors. How will you find different ways to be refreshed and enlivened?

Simply copying what someone else has done is no guarantee of success. You are unique, your situation is unique, and your hope will be unique. So how do you best find your unique way of hoping? You dabble. You experiment.

Begin by turning off your "interior judge," that part of you that so easily squashes untested ideas. Tell yourself, "No idea is silly if it gives me hope." Sometimes, in fact, it is that seemingly absurd thought that will *ignite* your hope. Gather all the creative notions you can, including the wild ones. If you want, ask others to join in. Then try out, one at a time, those ideas that hold some possibility. Keep those that work. Tinker with those that almost work. Drop those that fizzle. Smile at those that are best left untried.

Try one hope experiment today. Do another tomorrow. It won't be long before you have the hoping habit.

The little things are infinitely
the most important.

ARTHUR CONAN DOYLE

~

The one who removes a mountain
begins by carrying away small stones.

CHINESE PROVERB

~

Great things are not made by impulse,
but by a series of small things brought together.

VINCENT VAN GOGH

~

Make one small difference.

Hope is not about moving mountains. It's about moving one single stone, and then another. Hope is not about changing the world. It's about making a little difference in one part of the world.

Taking that first step, however small it may seem, is a big step. It frees you from feeling immobilized. It gives you confidence you can take more steps. It starts you on your way and gives you momentum. It is a law of human nature as well as physics that it takes the greatest effort to overcome inertia. After that, each consecutive step builds on the previous one.

Try asking yourself, "In my situation, what is one small step I can take?" If that step seems too much, then come up with another that's smaller still. Don't be concerned about starting with the "right" step – just start! And don't be concerned about having to make an impact on the problem you're facing – just do something that's manageable, something that feels satisfying after you've done it. Could you imagine picking up the telephone to call someone or getting out of your home to go somewhere? Perhaps your decision will be to start by cooking something simple, by eating something healthy, by fixing something broken, or by doing something relaxing. Maybe it's as basic as cleaning your room or making your bed. Maybe it's even more basic, like getting out of bed.

When you've made one small difference, you've taken a step forward. You've started to take control. Who knows where that will lead?

We are disturbed not by things,
but by the view we take of them.

EPICTETUS

~

The mind is its own place,
and in itself can make a Heav'n of Hell,
or a Hell of Heav'n.

JOHN MILTON

~

Learn to tilt.

"What's been funny about being a cancer patient this week?"

That question is asked regularly at the Center for Meaningful Life Therapy in Japan. It is an invitation to "tilt."

When you tilt, it's like cocking your head to one side. You look at things from a slightly different perspective. You see things in a little different light. Even the smallest tilt can make a noticeable difference in the feelings you experience and in the possibilities you may consider.

Asking questions you don't normally ask is a good way to practice tilting. It can also make room for hope. Here are some questions you might try:

What can I find that's humorous about this situation, if only for a few moments?

What are all the things I can name that are within my control?

What are the ways this situation might turn out better than I expected?

In what ways might this challenge be an opportunity?

What strengths can I develop here?

What lessons can I learn here?

If a very hopeful person were in my shoes, what is the first thing they would do? What would they do after that?

How will I describe this situation ten years from now?

Come up with your own questions that will lead you to do a "tilt." But don't stop there. Answer them.

I felt it shelter to speak to you.

EMILY DICKINSON

~

Tell me who you live with
and I will tell you who you are.

SPANISH PROVERB

~

Every friend represents a world in us,
a world possibly not born until they arrive,
and it is only by this meeting
that a new world is born.

ANAÏS NIN

~

Find good company.

Hope is contagious. So is hopelessness. That's why it's important to have hopeful people for companions.

Good companions care about you. They enjoy being around you. They encourage you to grow. They don't try to fix things in your life – they respect your ability to do that yourself. But they are there for you when you need them, including the tough times. Good companions don't center their life on yours. They find ways to fulfill many of their own needs and they give you space to fulfill yours. They believe in you. Count yourself fortunate if you have one or more good companions in your life now.

And what if you have some "no-hopers" in your world? You know what they're like. They don't believe in you and often they don't believe in hope itself. They're not open to the possibilities. They drag you down. You may need to put some physical or emotional distance between you and them. That's not always easy, especially if they are family members or close friends. But if you don't create a buffer for yourself, your hope will suffer.

Where do you find those companions who are good for your hope? In every walk of life. People who are great hopers hang out in all sorts of places, do every kind of work, and have every level of education. They can be any age, including the very youngest. Sometimes, in fact, the most infectious hopers are the youngest of all.

If you feel awkward seeking good company, remember that hopeful people like to share their hope. It's as natural for them as it is good for you.

Say what you have to say,
and not what you ought.

HENRY DAVID THOREAU

~

Every person's life is a fairy tale
written by God's fingers.

HANS CHRISTIAN ANDERSEN

~

If you do not tell the truth about yourself,
you cannot tell it about other people.

VIRGINIA WOOLF

~

Tell your story.

"To be a person is to have a story to tell," wrote the Danish author Isak Dinesen. She told her story so forcefully that it became a bestseller and the popular movie, *Out of Africa*. Her personal saga of love, loss, and hope became one with which many people could identify.

She was right: if you are a human being, then you have a story to tell. Your life is a series of unique tales. Communicating these stories helps your life begin to come together and make sense. In telling where you've been and where you now are, you can make connections you might not otherwise make. You also open the way for where you're going. When you do that, you open the way to hope.

When you take the time to tell your story, you convey that your story is worth being told, and worth being listened to. Placed together in this way, your smaller stories form your larger story, and that larger story carries the messages of your life:

"I have been a survivor and I'll survive again."

"I have learned and grown through the years, and I'm learning and growing still."

"My tale isn't finished – I have more stories to live and share."

Speaking your story is the most common way of telling it. But it's far from the only way. You can write it, perhaps as an autobiography, a journal, or a scrapbook. You can record it in pictures, in paint, in sound. You can pass your story on to those around you and to those who will follow you.

So go ahead. Start your tale and see where it takes you. Along the way, look for the messages it carries regarding what's becoming of your life.

The scholar seeks, the artist finds.

ANDRE GIDE

~

Every child is an artist.
The problem is how to remain an artist
once the child grows up.

PABLO PICASSO

~

I do believe it is possible to create,
even without writing a word or painting a picture,
by simply molding one's inner life.
And that too is a deed.

ETTY HILLESUM

~

Let out the artist.

The word "artist" brings to mind someone with a drawing pencil, a paintbrush, or a camera in hand. Yet there are many other ways to be creative. Some people are artists with garden tools, wrench sets, or wallpaper supplies. Others show their artistry in the kitchen, the sewing room, or the woodworking shop. Some are artists in their relationships, their volunteer efforts, or their chosen line of work. Some are quite accomplished at what they do, while others are artists in progress.

Something very fulfilling happens when you free the artist within. You follow your intuitions. You go where your energy leads. You open up. Often the situation you're facing seems to open up at the same time. And hope feels invited to return. It appears in the drawing you make, the music you create, the wood you polish, the plants you nurture, the words you write, the feelings you speak from the heart. While sometimes you're made aware of that hope right away, other times you don't see it until later.

Jack was a high profile businessman. He never figured he would be a candidate for early retirement due to illness. But cancer plays no favorites. One day family and friends presented him with a gift about which he had long fantasized – an oil painting set and an easel. After he completed his first painting, he stood back, amazed. He realized his beginner's strokes revealed quite a bit about him and his situation. More than that, he felt the best he had felt in a long while!

Give some thought to how you can best express yourself as the unique artist you are. What "artwork" might you begin today? Whatever medium you choose, you'll be taking the way of hope.

Against the onslaught of laughter,
nothing can stand.

SAMUEL CLEMENS

~

Humor is a prelude to faith,
and laughter is the beginning of prayer.

REINHOLD NIEBUHR

~

The most wasted of all days
is that during which one has not laughed.

SEBASTIAN-ROCH CHAMFORT

~

Let out the clown.

Have you heard the one about the newspaper photographer who took pictures of a man on his 99th birthday? Afterward the photographer said, "I hope I'll be here to celebrate your 100th with you." The old man replied, "I hope so too. But don't worry about it, son – you look pretty healthy to me."

Humor comes from the unexpected. Just when you think you know what will happen next, oops! – something else happens instead. You're caught off-guard, and you grin or chuckle or laugh out loud. You release that child-like clown within you that likes to giggle and have fun.

Humor is a wonder drug. It has its own pharmacy of natural painkillers and antidepressants that it shoots into your body by way of your brain. The more you laugh, the more of these natural drugs you give yourself. And they're all free!

Laughing helps reduce any tension you may feel. When you laugh at something, it's a way of stepping back and getting a broader perspective, a different look at things. That frees you to respond in ways you might otherwise not. It helps you bond with others who share these moments of fun with you. Undoubtedly, humor helps you hope.

You need hope in the very situations where you are tempted to say, "This is no laughing matter." How do you know that? Are you sure there isn't *something* worthy of humor here? Are you sure laughter would not help you see life in a brighter light?

So come up with material for the comedian within you. Tape up cartoons where you can see them. Read what's humorous. Write or say what's amusing. Watch what's hilarious. Spend time with people who tickle your funny bone. Ask others for their jokes. Tell your own. Be goofy. Let a wonderful twinkle form in your eye. When it does, hope will be forming too.

My yesterdays walk with me.

WILLIAM GOLDING

~

Memory is the mother of all wisdom.

AESCHYLUS

~

Hope is an echo,
hope ties itself yonder, yonder.

CARL SANDBURG

~

Keep a reminder nearby.

"A stone from Chapman Lake kept my hope alive," said Christen after being quizzed by her ordination committee. She knew her stance in favor of gay rights was unpopular, yet she also knew she had to be true to her convictions. She carried a stone from a favorite spot which had served as an oasis during some trying times of her life. With each rub of that stone, she remembered to stay calm and hope.

It's important to remember to hope. In times of adversity, there are usually plenty of reminders of the difficulties you face and the risks you run. That makes it all the more essential to give yourself reminders of the possibilities you have and the hopes you can harbor. Otherwise you may forget.

You can remind yourself simply to remain hopeful in general. Some people put inspiring photographs or paintings on their walls or desks. Some hang posters with cheering thoughts or carry notes with affirming words. A brightly-colored sun-catcher hanging in the window or a small treasure from nature placed on a table can also direct your thoughts toward hope. You may choose to use religious objects or symbols in a similar way. Whatever you choose, consciously say to yourself, "This is my reminder to hope."

You can also remind yourself of your specific hopes. If you're hoping for someone's healing, you might keep their picture close. If you're hoping for your own wholeness, you might direct your thoughts with a candle, a crystal, or a special piece of jewelry. If your hoping involves a relationship, you might place something that belongs to that other person in your pocket or purse, or use it as a bookmark or paperweight. A sound can also serve as a reminder. Each time a clock chimes, for example, you can treat it as a message calling out to you, "Hope!".

Wherever you are, whatever you are doing, there is a reminder that would work for you. Will you decide what it will be?

As long as you live, keep learning how to live.

SENECA

~

Practice is nine-tenths.

RALPH WALDO EMERSON

~

I know of no more encouraging fact
than the unquestionable ability of a person
to elevate their life by a conscious endeavor.

HENRY DAVID THOREAU

~

Practice. Then practice some more.

A concert pianist who does not rehearse? Absurd. An Olympic swimmer who refuses to train? Impossible. Learn to ride a bike or fly a plane without doing it over and over? Unrealistic. Become good at hope without practicing it? Not likely!

So how do you practice hope?

You practice by naming hope whenever and wherever you find it. When you see it in everyday events, in the actions of others, in the world around, you note it. You put up your antennae and you keep them up.

You practice by highlighting hope as you come across it. You can do that by pondering it, journaling about it, speaking of it, meditating on it.

You practice by taking hope in. You internalize the hopeful messages you find in the music you listen to, the movies you watch, the articles you read, the people you spend time with. You make conscious choices about what you see and hear.

You practice hope by expressing it. You tell yourself daily what you're hopeful about and what you're hoping for. You repeat stories of hope to others and to yourself.

You practice hope by preserving it. You keep a record of it, if only in your mind. You build a reservoir of hope so you can return to it when you want, so you can call upon it when you need. You keep your hope nearby and available.

When you practice your ability to hope, it becomes like any other skill you develop. You get better at it over time. You become stronger at doing it. You become more natural at showing it.

Who knows? By keeping at it, you may even become a pro.

When our hopes break,
let our patience hold.

THOMAS FULLER

~

Hope is patience with the lamp lit.

TERTULLIAN

~

Hold on; hold fast; hold out.
Patience is genius.

COMTE DE BUFFON

~

Develop patience.

As a young man Nelson Mandela, the Black lawyer and political activist, hoped that his native South Africa would become a democratic society with equal rights for all races. He took political action to bring that hope to reality. After he was arrested, sentenced, and silenced, he was forced to nurse that hope from a prison cell. He waited there almost thirty years, separated from his family and friends, before his hope came true. He was even named president of the land he loved.

Like Mandela, you may have to wait awhile for your hope to turn into reality. Are you prepared to do that? Most of us find it hard to wait. It feels unproductive. We like to see results, if not quickly, then within a reasonable period of time. But hope doesn't always work that way. Events are seldom predictable. Life will never be entirely under our control. Often, therefore, you must have patience as you hope. You may need to exercise that patience for a day, a month, a season, or many seasons. It may stretch out even longer.

The persistent inventor Thomas Edison had a saying: "Everything comes to those who hustle while they wait." In a sense, that's what hope is – a kind of hustling-while-waiting. You keep holding on to your hope, and you polish it as you do so. You may refine your hope as times change or as you change. Being patient, however, does not mean putting your life on hold while you wait. Hoping with patience means living as fully as possible given the circumstances life has handed you or you have chosen. It means accepting that sometimes things may not go your way. It means understanding that oftentimes a deep hope can come true even if your smaller hopes do not.

Hoping is seldom an overnight success. It's more like a lifetime adventure.

Begin at once to live,
and count each day as a separate life.

SENECA

~

We should consider every day lost
in which we have not danced at least once.

FRIEDRICH NIETZSCHE

~

Those who bring sunshine to the lives of others
cannot keep it from themselves.

JAMES M. BARRIE

~

Celebrate.

Ten years after Allen's open heart operation, Ronna hosted a party to celebrate the hope they had lived during those added years together. Jim threw a surprise birthday party for his wife Bernie one year to the day after her surgery for cancer. He wanted to make up for the birthday she missed the year before, so those who loved her could say in person, "We're glad your hoping is paying off."

When you celebrate, you communicate something is important enough to be highlighted or someone is valued enough to be fussed over. It's a way of expressing gratitude and appreciation. It's a way of showing love.

Birthdays, anniversaries, and graduations are all occasions that can honor how people's hopes have come true and are continuing to come alive. Yet there are many other kinds of events that call out to be celebrated. Recuperation from a serious illness or injury is worth formally marking somehow. So is healing after a loss. But why stop there? Why not celebrate those significant steps you take all along the way? Why not make occasions to celebrate the people who support you, the blessings that surprise you, the experiences that lift you? Why not celebrate hope itself – how it keeps you going, how it adds to your life?

It doesn't take much to celebrate. You can do it with a special meal, a thoughtful gift, a personal note, or perhaps some spoken words you've prepared. While celebrations work especially well when others are involved, you can also do it by yourself with your own little ritual, or by giving yourself a favorite treat, or by spending time in a special place.

When you celebrate, you say, "Look how fortunate!". Whatever has happened, whatever is happening, you encourage your own hope when you take time to acknowledge the fortune that is yours and to mark how far you've come.

The one who has a why *for life*
can put up with any how.

FRIEDRICH NIETZSCHE

~

This time, like all times, is a very good time,
if we but know what to do with it.

RALPH WALDO EMERSON

~

To live is to suffer.
To survive is to find meaning in the suffering.

VIKTOR FRANKL

~

Look for the meaning.

Viktor Frankl encountered hope while imprisoned in a WWII concentration camp. He was marching one winter morning, cold, weak, and depressed. The man beside him said, "If only our wives could see us now!" Frankl began to imagine his wife, imprisoned in another camp. He saw her smile vividly. He felt her encouraging him to go on. He experienced her love for him and his for her with a depth he had not known, even when they were side by side. He later said he survived those frightful conditions because of his hope they'd be reunited.

When you tie your hope to something that really matters to you, you have more energy and endurance to move forward. When something is really important to you, it gives your life meaning. This meaning is not so much *outside* you as *inside* you. It's very personal.

Ask yourself, "What really matters to me?" Is it your love for someone? Is it your desire to leave something that will outlast you? Is it your commitment to do what you believe is right? What matters to you doesn't need to be grand in scale. Maybe it's a quiet wish you've held but haven't spoken about. Maybe it's related to an honored pet or a newly-found friendship. Maybe it's your desire to put to good use something unfortunate that has happened to you.

As for Frankl, when the war ended, he learned his wife had already died. While his grief was deep, he held on to a sense of meaning. He wove her memories and her love into a new hope he created for his life. He hoped he could teach others to choose their own attitude toward what happens to them, just as he had learned to do. Eventually his hope came true and the book he wrote of his experiences is now considered one of the most helpful ever written for those low on hope.

Search for what's meaningful in your life and right next to it you'll find what gives you hope.

Invited or not, God is present.

INSCRIPTION ABOVE DOORWAY
IN CARL JUNG'S HOME

~

Behold! A sacred voice is calling you!
All over the sky a sacred voice is calling!

BLACK ELK

~

There are only two ways to live your life.
One is as though nothing is a miracle.
The other is as if everything is.

ALBERT EINSTEIN

~

Open to what's sacred.

"Now there are some things we all know. We all know that *something* is eternal. And it ain't houses, and it ain't names, and it ain't earth, and it ain't even stars." Those words are spoken by the stage manager in *Our Town*, Thornton Wilder's classic play about ordinary life in a small community. People who hope have an inkling what he's talking about. Deep in our bones we feel that something eternal exists. Something sacred is around us. We may have words to put to this experience, or we may not. We may be clear about the place of the sacred in our lives, or we may be less sure. We may even doubt it at times. Hope does not promise all the answers. Rather, it accepts that some answers are unknowable. Through it all, hope remains open to that mystery that is around us.

People connect with the sacred in various ways. You may turn to scriptures, worship, prayer, or meditation. You may do this alone or with others. You may do this routinely or as you feel called. You may make this connection in less obvious ways – by taking slow walks in nature, for instance, or by reading something, whatever its title, that draws you inward and outward at the same moment. Sometimes simply staying in silence for awhile grounds you spiritually.

Hoping is not the same as praying, although hope can be woven into your prayer. It is not a matter of feeling especially sacred, although in looking back you can sometimes sense sacredness was at the center of your hope. When you stay hopeful, you remain open to the possibility that there is more than just this physical world and more than just this present moment. You grant that something greater may be at work around you and even within you. And that something greater may be Something Greater.

My hopes are not always realized
but I always hope.

OVID

~

It is always morning somewhere.

HENRY WADSWORTH LONGFELLOW

~

Hope is not the conviction
that something will turn out well,
but the certainty that something makes sense,
regardless of how it turns out.

VACLAV HAVEL

~

Live as if.

George's family had just learned the seriousness of his cancer. They asked the surgeon, "Should we tell him the facts so he can deal with the reality of his situation?" She responded wisely, "*Which* reality?"

That doctor was right. There's the reality of the statistical tables: "Chances are one in ten he'll survive six months." But there's also the reality behind those statistics: for each ten, one survives; for each thousand, one hundred live. Then there's the reality of the man himself: What will he do to improve his chances? What will he hope for? And will he be one who survives? That possibility is as viable as the other. It's not as likely but it's just as real.

There is no such thing as false hope. Any hope you carry is real hope. If your hope is different than those around you, it simply means you're focusing on a reality which may not be their reality. Perhaps yours is based upon something that happened in your past, or something you know about yourself that's unquestionably true. Perhaps what's real for you is informed by the accounts of others who beat the odds. You may see the same data everyone else sees, yet still choose to place your hope on the long shot.

Whatever the odds, they're only odds. Can you beat them? Who knows? The important question is, are you willing to live as if beating the odds is a real possibility? Are you ready to live as if what you hope for can come true, even if all the evidence isn't in yet?

Will you live as if you have something to live for? And will you commit to hoping while you live?

Seize the day.

HORACE

~

Cry. Cry if you must.
But do not complain.
The path has chosen you.
And in the end you will say,
Thank you.

DAG HAMMARSKJÖLD

~

Say "yes."

No one plans to develop a chronic illness. No one expects to be the victim of an accident or some other tragedy. No one starts out life with a goal of being unemployed, or disabled, or unhappily alone. But such things happen. Life does not always turn out the way you wish. When that happens, what are you to do? Live with it? Fight it? Ignore it? Give in to it? There may be reason to take any of these stances at one time or another. The hopeful response, however, is different.

Hope says "yes." Yes, whatever has happened, there will be ways to handle it. Yes, whatever has been handed you, you can deal with it. Yes, the unexpected can bring joy as well as sorrow. Misfortune can be a cause for growth as well as for grief.

Hope says, "Yes, life can still be good." Hope does not say this easily or blithely or even conditionally. It's not a matter of "*Yes, if my health holds out,*" or "*Yes, if our relationship works,*" or "*Yes, if what I want comes true.*" Hope is a matter of saying "yes" with no strings attached. Just "yes."

Living that "yes" means believing that if today is not the way you want it to be, tomorrow can be a another story. Something new and different can happen. The difference may be in the situation, in others, or in yourself. It doesn't matter. What matters is there *can be* a difference and that difference is real.

Have you said "yes" to life before? Can you call upon the strength of that experience to say it again? If you haven't spoken this "yes," can you at least believe it's possible to speak it? Will you try it at least once? Will you ask others to support you? Will you support yourself?

The wonder of hope is that your "yes" can even become a "YES!"

God asks no person
whether they will accept life.
That is not the choice.
You must take it.
The only choice is how.

HENRY WARD BEECHER

~

Live all you can;
it is a mistake not to.
It doesn't so much matter
what you do in particular,
so long as you have had your life.

HENRY JAMES

~

Afterword

Can hope ever become a way of life? Can it be the first place to which you return when challenge presents itself? Yes, we believe it can. It may take time for that to happen, more time than you wish. Initially it may take more effort than you'd like. As this way of being becomes more natural, you will begin to see the world through a particular lens – the lens of hope. You will feel an increasing confidence in your ability to turn to hope when uncertainty threatens your days. You will experience an increasing openness to allowing hope into more and more aspects of your life. You will come, in short, to live from a place of hope. You will come to make hope your home.

Do you remember as a child heading home for words of comfort when you bruised a knee or confronted the limits of being little in some other way? Do you remember the feeling of being able to regroup there? And if this could not happen in your physical home, can you remember what else helped you head back into the big world? Fortified with the experience of having a safe haven in which you could gather yourself together, you felt more hopeful you could handle the next steppingstones that awaited you.

That's what it's like to make hope your home.

The opposite of this is to make fear your home. Then you spend large portions of your days being afraid of what might happen. You go about your life presuming the worst is just waiting to occur. You convey these expectations to others. At every turn you deny the possibilities.

When you live your life from the place of hope, you find yourself frequently thinking of how things might turn out well. Even as you face new and uncertain circumstances, you find yourself asking questions like these: "In my situation, what would a hopeful person do?" "Given what I'm facing, what is the best thing that might happen?" "If the short-term future isn't going to be to my liking, what about the long-term?"

As you learn to live life in this way, you help hope become a habit. As you acquire and use the hope strategies that work especially well for you, you learn to trust the process more and more. You will trust yourself more and more too. As your attitude of hope grows stronger, it becomes second nature for you to return to that hopeful stance when you sometimes venture away from it.

Although your hope may flicker at times, it will not be snuffed out entirely. Although you may not always see the way ahead clearly, you will continually be reminded by signs around you that hope is real and it's never far away. The voice in your head will echo the encouragement you need. When challenges come your way, you will treat them as one more episode in the unfolding story of your hope. The random acts of kindness you give and receive will no longer feel so random. When you speak, your voice will carry the tenor of hope. When you reach out, it will be with the touch of hope. When you act, it will be with the spirit of hope.

When you live this way, you will be ready to reach out for a hope loan when that's necessary, neither embarrassed to need it nor afraid to borrow it. You will realize that if a particular hope strategy doesn't help you today, something else will help you tomorrow. Or the day after. Or the day after that.

As you center yourself in your place of hope, you will understand the power that can come with making one small difference in your life. You will understand the importance of surrounding yourself with people who can be positive and influences that are healthy. You will remember the significance of looking back as the first step in looking forward. You will commit yourself to practicing your hope. You will encourage yourself to be patient as you hope. You will validate yourself by saying "yes" to life and "yes" to hope every chance you get.

By living your life more and more this way, you will notice that it will become less and less important for things always to turn out well or to turn out exactly as you wish. You will come to believe that you will be okay and life can be good no matter *how* things turn out. Sometimes you will still hurt. You will still grieve. You can still be disappointed. But you will know your bruises can heal. You will know this because you will have a home you can return to when you need it. That home will be your hope. And it will make all the difference.

Ronna Jevne is a professor, psychologist, lecturer, and writer well known for her work in the area of hope. She is program director of the Hope Foundation of Alberta whose mission is to study and enhance hope as it relates to health and education. She can be contacted at

The Hope Foundation of Alberta
11032 - 89 Avenue
Edmonton, Alberta, Canada T6G 0Z6
780/492-9811 and 780/492-9813 (fax)
ronna.jevne@ualberta.ca
www.ualberta.ca/~natashar

James E. Miller is a grief counselor, clergyman, writer/photographer, and lecturer who presents in the areas of loss and grief, older age, caregiving, managing transition, and spirituality. He is the founder of Willowgreen Productions, Willowgreen Publishing, and Willowgreen Consulting. He may be contacted at

Willowgreen
P.O. Box 25180
Fort Wayne, Indiana 46825
219/424-7916 and 219/426-3002 (fax)
jmiller@willowgreen.com
www.willowgreen.com